HOW TO BE A SUPER KID

Written & Illustrated
by Abigail E. Perez

Printed in the United States of America

First Printing, 2018

ISBN 978-1-7329180-0-9

www.howtobeasuperkid.com

This book is dedicated to
Brianna Greenspan and Nick Santonastasso

There is no such thing as an unimportant superhero with a useless superpower. Everyone has a superpower. When you find yours, use it to change the world one person at a time.

-Abigail Perez

CALLING ALL SUPERS!

Congratulations on taking the first step towards a life-long journey of developing your super kid gifts and abilities! We have a special community we would like to invite you and your grown ups to be a part of where you can connect, learn and grow with other amazing super kids! Join us in the super kid movement and become the super kid you were created to be! After you read this book, as part of your first mission, post a video of yourself saying the super kid creed and inspire your friends and others to step up to the #superkidchallenge.

Visit us on-line at www.howtobeasuperkid.com.

You are invited to join the super kid troop!
Here is the required six layered scoop...

Scoop number 1:
Let's get started with the fun.

Every super kid has
a super routine.
It helps your heart
stay pure and clean.

Abigail's Super Routine

6:00 am   Rise & Shine

6:20 am   Healthy Breakfast

6:40 am   Affirmations

6:50 am   Devotional/Journal

7:00 am   Exercise at bus stop

7:40 am   School

Early to bed, early to rise.

Helps your mind become sharp and wise.

Find time to read the Bible
or other inspiring works.
It's a powerful way to squash
a negative thought that lurks.

Scoop number 2:
Take notes so you
know what to do.

Every super kid has special powers.
And it doesn't require knocking down towers.

If a bully is mean
and calls you a name...

Turn away from the bully
but don't act the same.

Remember the affirmations from
the start of your day.
Hold on to these truths
as you go on your way.

Abigail's affirmations

I am beautifully and
wonderfully made.

I choose to be happy!

I am confident.

I am kind.

I am victorious!

Scoop number 3:
Adjust your focus
so you know what to see.

Always, always give it your best...

But never ever compare with the rest.

Sometimes in life
we will have to take risks.
While the outcome may be uncertain
the chance to learn still exists.

Don't be discouraged if you happen to fail.
It may take many tries before you set sail.

Scoop number 4:
Listen closely if you want to learn more.

Take care of your mind, body, and soul.
You will need all three to reach your ultimate goal.

Don't forget to eat
your protein, veggies and fruit.
It's a must if you want
to earn your super suit.

Make time to exercise.
You can play, dance or run.
You can do it with some friends.
It's always a lot of fun!

Scoop number 5:
You're ready to take the dive.

26

Create stretch goals by raising the bar.
It's the path that leads to the gold star!

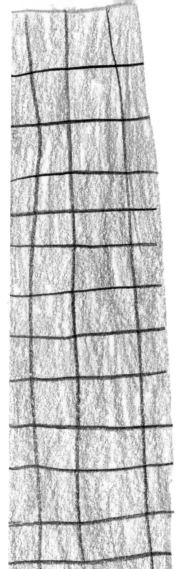

When life gets hard and you hit a wall
don't get discouraged from the fall.
Pick yourself up and do not fear.
Press on, your breakthrough is near.

Scoop number 6:
Spread happiness by adding SHINE to the mix!

Invest in those who help you grow
by being part of their front row.

Make today your day to shine.
Why wait for tomorrow?
There's no better time.

Now apply the things
that you have learned,
and celebrate the super kid status
that you have earned.

SUPER KID TRAITS

Self-control
Unique
Problem solver
Empathetic
Respectful

Kind

Imaginative

Determined

SUPER KID CREED

I am proud to be a super kid!
I will be kind and compassionate.
I will learn from my mistakes.
I will show self-control and respect.
I will never bully anyone in any way.
I will use my gifts and talents to make
the world a better place.
I will shine bright by making
front row moments.
I am committed to be the super kid
I was created to be.

_____ _____
Sign   Date